PURSUIT

FREEDOM
REVELATIONS

PENEMUE

Outskirts Press, Inc.
http://www.outskirtspress.com

ISBN: 978-1-4787-4015-5

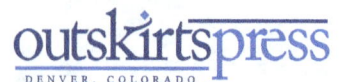

Outskirts Press and the "OP" logo are trademarks belonging to Outskirts Press, Inc.

PRINTED IN THE UNITED STATES OF AMERICA

For my wonderful girls,
you are my guiding light on my way home,
always.

Contents

Introduction

Life is an inspiring force. There are many sources of great inspiration in this world. Our natural world within planet earth is diverse and complex. Life is truly the most inspiring element. Our lives as humans however are completely unique in their synthesized departure from the natural world. For example we humans have these little things called ideas and dreams. Our main source of conflict is usually the difference within our ideas and dreams, this alone is the source of so much discord within the human race as a species.

No other creature has our unique problem or the very distinct capability of language to solve these problems. I have always used language to find reason and resolution. However, expressions are perhaps the greatest use of language I can think of within humanity. Expression is the force that either: heals, hurts, unites, divides, conquers, surrenders, builds, destroys and or creates. Language is our law, poetry, history, and science. I wrote this selection of poetry in order to express divides as well as in the hope of uniting. To express our inability to surrender our ideas and to remember the law and history as they once were upheld and honored. I hope it creates a source of inspiration for you and yours. It is my vivid depiction of a vision in regards to the nation today contrasted to what once was along with ominous warning signs of what might be.

Our expressions are our most valued possessions in this our great existence. Our freedom to express our perspectives and thoughts is more precious than gold. Many men have sacrificed their lives for this one thought and ideal. Therefore we must honor those who have had the foresight to bestow and ensure our tongues and minds remain free to heal, unite, defy, and inspire. I welcome you to inspire someone today, tomorrow and always!

Liberty continuously escapes humanity. It is the angel that saves us in the most dire of hours and in the darkest of battles. It is the element within the human spirit that will never be vanquished. It will never be silenced, never be controlled, never be destroyed or eliminated. It is a force which is impossible to eradicate with hate or any other tool or device.

It is the one and only true lasting legacy we can leave our children on this earth.

In the name of the *fallen* and all those who may still fall in the battle for our great cause of freedom and independence.

PENEMUE

PURSUIT

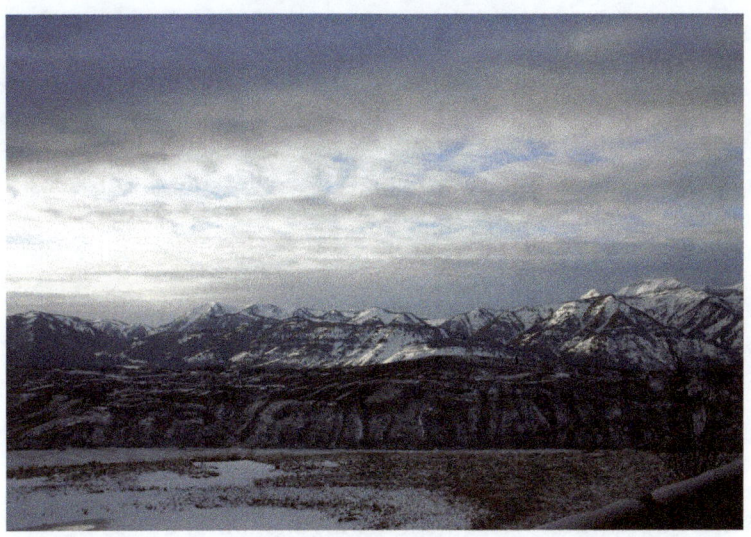

In the pursuit of the most righteous definitions of human
       existence, sometimes the human condition requires
resistance.

Challengers of the status quo, those brave few intellectuals
who would want to know. Those who set forth at the task at
hand, ask the tough questions and break with the band.

Those who betray the betrayers. Insiders from· the
collective
       of misbehavers. Born again, tell all repentance
players. Freedom remains aloof, a fight will take flight that
will require every last nail and tooth.

Generational loss of prosperity and identity due to
totalitarian

propensity, multitudes of humanity inherently
herded.

Foundations of freedom in upheaval we are under attack
from
      a truly great evil. A new age is drawing. This
impasse has no bridge drawing. Irreconcilable differences
much more than mere hindrances.

Extremist radicals from the perspective of each other and
what
      they envision. Clearly there exists a massive state
of division. Its derision obvious to all those not blinded by
greed and denial. Set forth the guilty verdict and trail by
fire. An ignition worse than the inquisition of our age.
      Finish setting the stage.
Soon the crowd will gather and set it a blaze.

In the pursuit of all that is beholden to the righteous
believers of mans right to choose, decide, dissent try our
best and repent.

God will remain when all else is fallen and crumbling
      come and gather around the light
the angels trumpet is calling.

SOVEREIGNTY

The island is my nation. Independence my own creation.
Rules within abound but outside opinions
are way out of bounds.

A global collective of the dually
elected.
They oppress indiscriminately most all are selected.
Violations of international law, secret courts rule man with
an eye that sees all.

Foreign nations perspective of the American intrusion are
putrid as if a poisonous infusion.

Friends have been betrayed in this our great age of
fear
and confusion.

Freedom seems lost in a delusion or simply
mere illusion.

My island is my nation and so without hesitation
this is my exclamation of proclamation.
Independence from the establishment titans
ruling
our lives like tyrants.

Welfare for those who do not care. Handouts all
around

apathy abounds, reality torn to shrouds. Liquidity an
absurdity
    Integrity an insecurity.

            Oath of the defenders, reduced to that of
    global
elitist pretenders.
            Violated foreign sovereignty has severed
    relations.
Sanctions placed on nations with no thought of other
peaceful persuasions.
            Colonial arrogance fills the air. Global
intoxication boils over in frustration,

                  over U.S. INTERVENTION

JUDGES

Establishment juggernauts shudder at the thought of
freedom by negotiating with those who perpetuate a system
of criminal misinformation, our civil liberties manipulation
and their expanded powers exaltation.

      Power corrupts and absolute power corrupts
absolutely. Totalitarianism has destroyed constitutionalism.

      Infiltration within every sector, freedom is
being eaten by Hannibal Lecture.

      Whole segments of our population are
persecuted for defending liberty

      and all she has executed.

First and second amendment trampled. Caesars men decide
who will fire and speak, tyrannical desire of a population
that is weak.

      Legacy of discontentment and lies the truth
of their failure will be burnt into our children's eyes.
History will not forget! My hope is the next generation will
make choices they will not regret.

      All record of man would have to be erased
in order to repeat these actions which have been disgraced.

   Targeted for elimination, prosecution then extermination.
Compromise a word no longer used. Minority squashed and
abused.

      Division their ultimate derision. Hatred and
envy their envoy for change. Violence they propel as they
sell them the rage.

      Unconstitutional decrees passed through a
senate that seethes about broken centuries old law, criminal
arrogance both stolen and flawed.

TECHNOCRATS
&
Tyrants

Soldiers and slaves but no free men to be had the founders vision vanished.

Technocracy rules the nation, new gadgets thrown down to the population.

Big brother surveillance, their eyes assail us. Tag, track and hack us they collect every fact of us.

Control of the masses is the goal. Masses of data worth more than gold, all in their control.

The social engineers of the era sitting atop fantastic thrones of terror.

Cyber empire of nuclear perfection sovereignty to be had or annihilation for intervention freedom from outside interjection.

Restrictions on encryption an unintelligent wound of self infliction they betray all security in exchange for innocents data descriptions.

Patriots and pirates, tea party compatriots and liberty conservatives speak freely your thoughts sincerely reserved for this sensation known as foreign corporate occupation.

Reasonable privacy expectations of the media that carries the lifeblood of our information, they have lied and stolen our lives without hesitation.

Outed by the guilt of one of their own, pain and aggravation caused to a nation disowned.

Scandals amidst a murderous agenda, disinformation used as factual intelligen-CIA.

Deny, deny, deny as the rest of the world decries. Evidence in hand, disdain for Uncle Sam all this time running a global totalitarian scam.

DIVINE PROVIDENCE

Pilgrim pride long lost and forgotten, policies of old distorted and rotten.

Foundations crumble, divine providence is proving evidence of injustice amongst mankind, misguided pride cut short their stride.

Fortunes of fortitude, wealth in strength of character and attitude.

Built a nation so high in its magnitude no other before it has reached these heights with such aptitude.

Guiding spirit of light, a constitution in sight, spiritual warriors expressing their fight. A new nation will be born from this plight.

Line in the sand against the monarch it stands. Options granted in this new land. Choices in the new world on how to express their voices, now they sing to the lord as they wish, everyone rejoices.

Moral, godly values forged a population of prosperous avenues. Free thinking founders created well-being not just,

Revenue.

ASSOCIATION
OF
FREEDOM

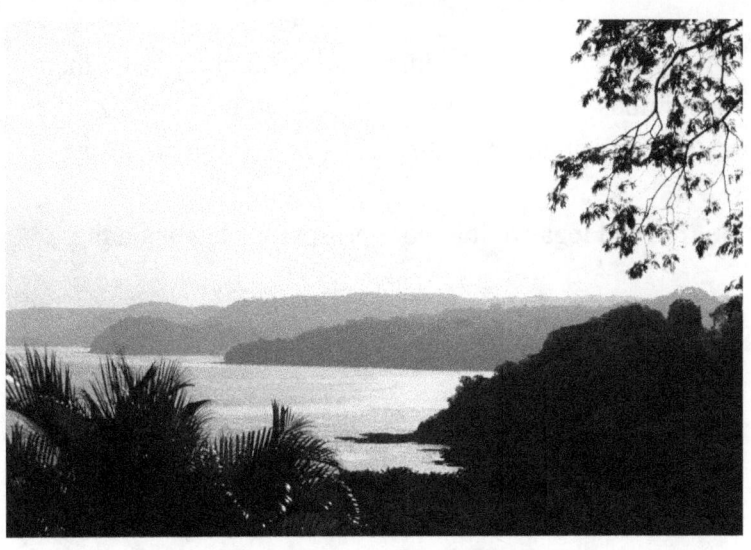

No noble royals only elitists who foil liberty for the average their appetite for power vicious and savage.

Navigation through higher elevations in a forest of segregation individually resisting subjugation.

An association of liberty forged in the soul of a
      lone individual. The group factor is residual, follow
      yourself, man in the mirror is the visual.

      In this new transition we must break free from our subservient position. No central colony or hive we are the sovereign creatures of earth, feel the vibe.

Statue in the wind that refuses to bend, never broken no need to mend.

Liberty gave me a kiss and told me to ride with the wind, I have not seen her since.

Aging, oxidizing, deteriorating faster than most minds are able to metabolize it. let me verbalize it, a restoration is underway the past won't be thrown away.

Be free and legalize it a more prosperous day is on the

way.

Father
TIME

Revolutionary changing of the guard. New resembles the old, comparably.

Our youth are peaceful and transparent the past is violent its lies apparent.

Our fathers fought against collectivism only for them to invoke socialism.

Revision of reality, historical perspectives distorted insanity.
Reaffirmations of free society reinforced by our fathers tongue. Stories of a youth fighting political oppression since he was young.

This is a multigenerational stand!

Prosperous salt in our food their desire is bland...

Focus through the storm the evil presumes! Within every new conflict more bodies exhumed. Into the fumes they burn, endless concentrations waiting their turn.

Elitist monopolies driving forces of history into profitable slaughter at the edict of evil sons and daughters.

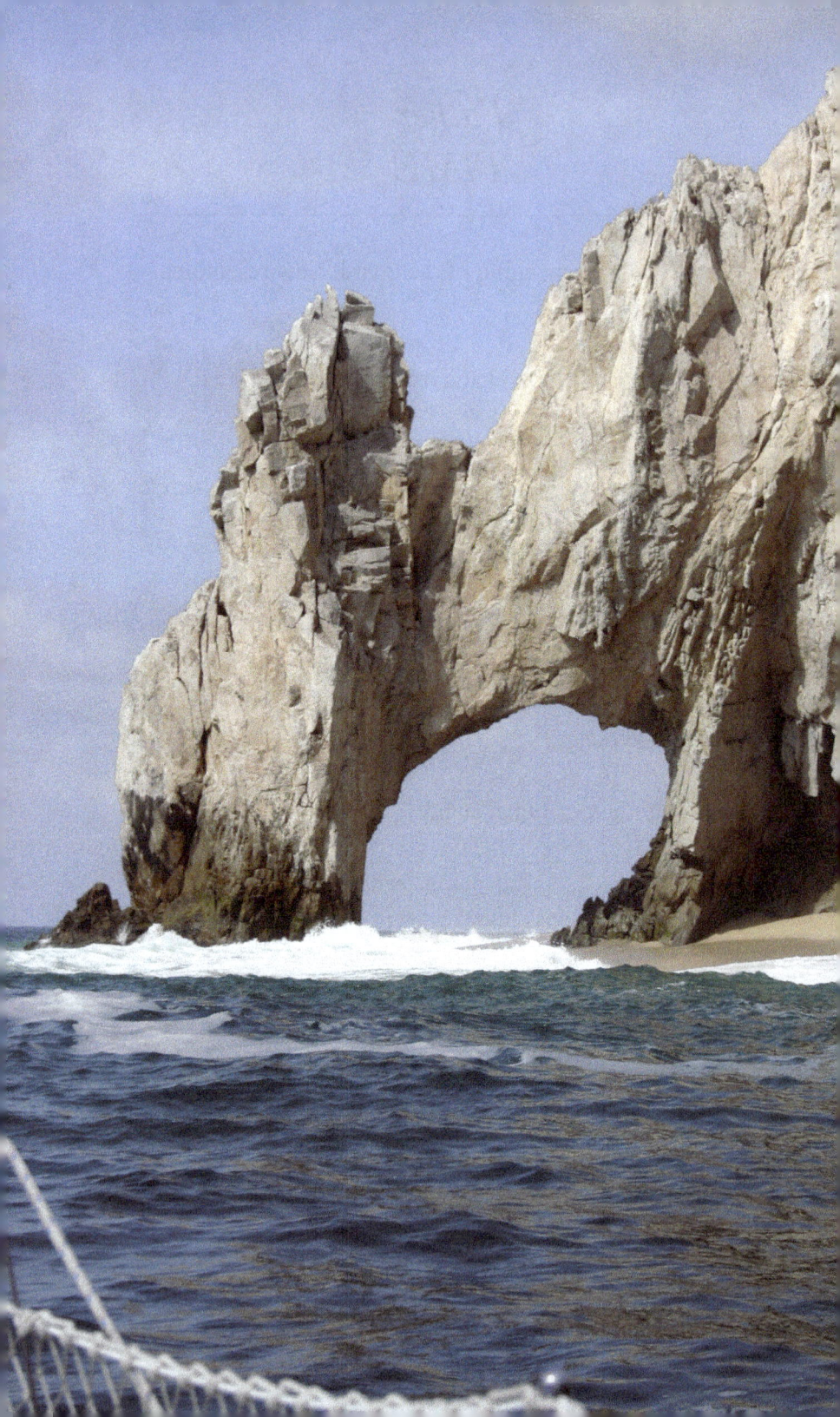

Turn over their coffers and refuse the debt they have to offer! War is the only thing they ever bring forth, the entire earth they will scorch.

Freedom, liberty and justice are forsaken in the presence of mere loans for trinkets. Who could ever think it? Life itself neglected for petty objects in a new imprisoned generation this is our own misguided integration.

FUTURE
CROP

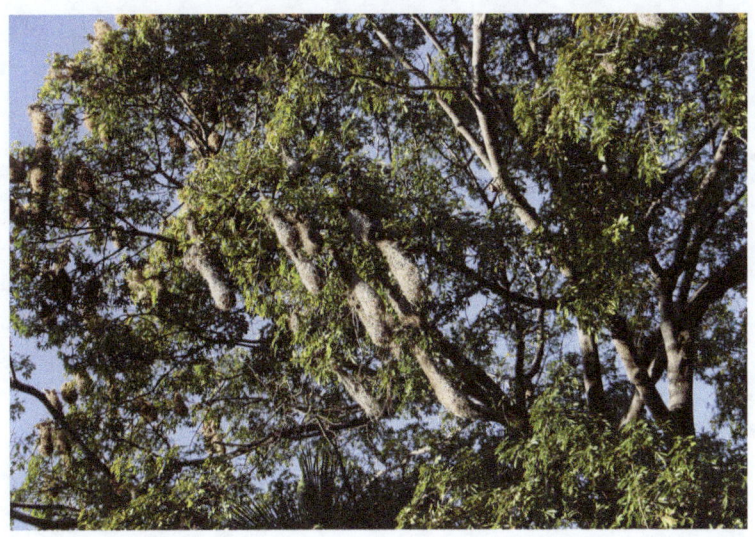

A gift so dear, all my love wishes to give you a life without
   fear.

A world where you can fly from branch to branch without
ever
   being shot down, follow your heart and discover your
dreams.

Inevitably there will be missiles shot up at you by their
   dismissals of your right to flight on your own path and
   not the fabricated mesh known as their scam.

The sacred rights guaranteed by your fathers to always
remain free
   will live in your spirit.

You will grow and you will sow, you will reap the crops
that will let you know.
Liberty is yours forever, no need to overthrow.

Let us celebrate our independence and ignite the flame,
there are new heights to discover and claim.

In you the rebellion wins, forgive them for their sins.
This war is fought every generation by those who
fly high against collectivist social degeneration and the
totalitarian arrogance of pompous indignation.
Set course, follow your dreams! Start your own nation
for those in the pursuit of happiness and innovative
creations.

A place like this exists but you must be tenacious and
persist,
no matter how much they resist you have a sacred right
to
exist.

Re-education and confiscation will not be crimes
committed
against your generation.
you must lift yourselves up to higher elevations never fall
asleep and always react to all

VIOLATIONS.

SYMBIOTIC
PLANET

Symbiotic elements come together to create man, man recombines elements to destroy nature and its plan. Creations last stand is under attack by all that we refuse to acknowledge and lack.

Light energy recombining elements into life, an eons long process is the time worth the fight?

Supreme being emerges to understand the light but light has many refractions through an atmosphere of earthly distractions.

All that glitters is not gold many will purchase it yet others are not sold.

What prophetic stories will you be told?

Will you fall for climate change or read and know on how there exists an agenda of deranged politicians who manipulate data like magicians?

Synergy creates the possibility for new entities. Diversity exists within a tolerant environment. Mankind destroys all as if a species squall, mostly just by lying about it all!

Radioactive, nuclear omissions a dying segment of ocean we the people have our suspicions.

Political agenda rules the facts, scientists pushed back,
silenced and oppressed for their work honestly expressed.

Falsehoods created to control with distress while other
truths are hidden and dismissed in the mess.

EXPLICIT
SCIENCE

Explicit science used against those in defiance. Wigs upon makeup masks it is a world for which no one really asks.

Psychological operations within technocratic tactics, freedom prevails at the end of my synopsis.

Radio waves and x-rays could not begin to explain what is in our DNA that make us behave this way.

Fearless and tenacious, this insubordination to them is outrageous.

Labeled us traitors and tyrants it is they who are the pirates. In our homes details in disguise our lives consumed by these spies they play a viscous game of lies. Our lives are transmitted for them to analyze.

Highest global prison population our price for non-compliance is ultimate subjugation.

America is a modern day plantation being driven by scientific exploitation used against the people for total control of the nation.

No technology that cannot be manipulated. Privacy lost due to timid hesitation. Whistleblowers are persecuted while the criminals create a station. A death star of occupation imbedded in isolation, what a truly destructive creation.

Categorized and cataloged just in case you did anything wrong or in the event that they wish to control you strong, liberty is now gone. A triage of espionage, sheer carnage, lives ravaged nothing left to salvage.

Agency upon agency, no more mob all in exchange for a government that robs. Intimidated and spooked they microwave and nuke. (*SSSS)*

Assimilate the metaphors! Words are better than guns for settling scores. Defund the N.S.A. and the rest of these whores.

Propagated and instigated, explicitly corrupt, lives regurgitated by violated science erupt.

Will we be able to break free in this my verbal proliferation or will we be a furthermore enslaved Population?

STATISM

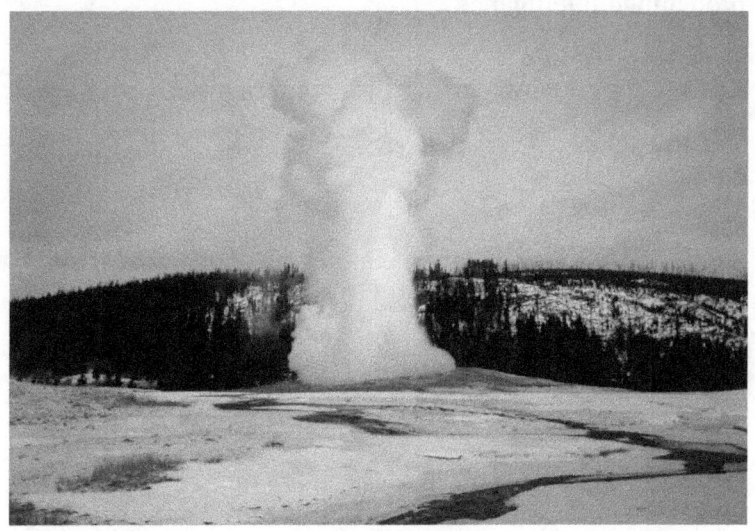

The state of the prison they all gather in support of the prism.
Knowing full well that public anger swells.

Many in alliance forming associations of defiance inspiration from freedom our only reliance.

All actions made illegal, existence is defiance.
Former priest of the state excommunicated and proclaimed a mistake but I would stake the claim it is they who deserve the blame.

New rebels on the scene demonized and demeaned.
Men who cannot be bought for if ever a vision justice sought.

Olympic sized pools filled with blood of those who fought for independence. They oppress all with their proclaimed intelligence.

Congressional committees omitting the truth from our cities. Our representatives misinformed while interests create treasonous reform.

The American people are being sold up the river. We need the truth to stand and deliver!

Bills past to cover the bankers bet, they have stolen our lives and sweat. Gamblers of a trade, bankers should meet the blade.

Justice will rise against all they comprise in order to liberate the people from it all when it finally falls.

Our minds are like a prison they have imprisoned us within the

Prism.

THE GREAT DEGENERATION

The so called great generation has given us ninety five years of social degeneration.

Every aspect of society controlled by welfare and impropriety regardless of our diversity or proprietary self-reliance.

To exist within one self without their parasitic invasion is considered a grave perversion.

Only the few exist bravely in this the great subversion. It is a submersion of past convictions. What remains they seek out for eviction but we are far from extinction.

We shall strive to revive principles of the past even as we barley survive.

We are the dreamers of the dreams living in a nation ripped at the seams.

War gave them purpose and pride. All along they were being taken for a ride.

Powers that be entrenching youths in the muck so the global industrial complex can make a bloody buck.

Not so great were they who would rather see their seeds in debt as long as they continue to get paid. Wrong even now as they fade.

Millennials standing up refusing to be neutered and spayed. We are not animals easily betrayed. We are the future of humanity not pawns to be played.

I have stated our case eloquently without profanity but what you deserve is insult for this fallacy, fabricated fantasy. War, war, war you continue to ask for more.

Do you not see how many are poor? War on poverty also manifested as loss never bested.

War on drugs eliminating the hugs, everyone labeled as a junky or thug. A plethora of selection no thanks to government objection.

Our path has been chosen by *wiser* men of centuries past whose enduring spirit will in us assuredly
LAST.

LAND OF OUR FATHERS

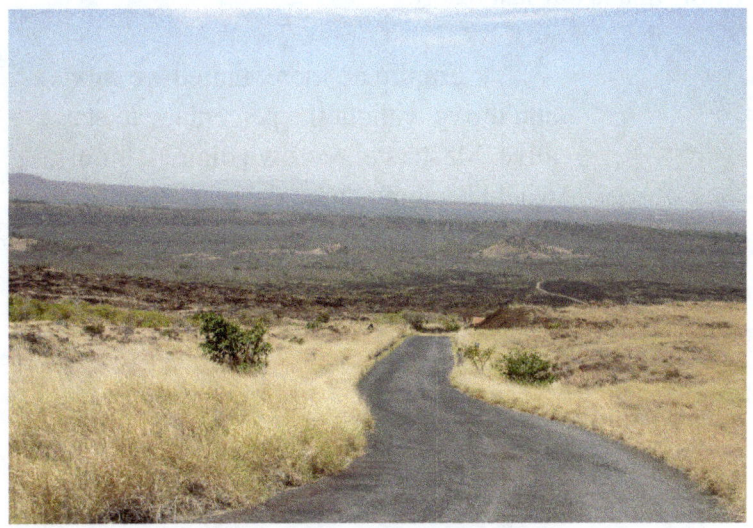

There no kings of this land only shepherds.
   Tyrants will arise and for freedom sake we will seek
their demise.

           The republic lives in our hearts if nowhere
else. Statism is another ploy intending to destroy the
impending fruit of freedom and its joy.

           A Stranglehold on humanity has been
      placed.
Constitutional ideas outpaced, all is regulation laced.

           Simply stated they are hyper-inflated.
Noxious like gasses created by false infusions, no more free
markets only confusion.
           Revolution and rebellion the only viable
      solutions.

With enough support we need a tax revolt! Do not let them extort this is our last resort.

> Empire no more, united we survive
> and thrive without the percentage to stay
> alive. Masters of our own dime! It surely
> would be about damn time.

MANIPULATION
OF THE SHEEPLE

Markets enrolled and controlled, governments bought and
sold.
    Souls lost to the power of greed & empire.
    War is their need and sole desire in order to distract
    you from the fires that burn. Serfs to a system which
does not
    learn to teach or allow you to earn so you can reach.
    We must discern for ourselves which lies to swallow
    and which impostors to follow.

        Lead us not into temptation and deliver us
        from evil. Injustices without accountability
        failure, corruption and crime the only
        reliability.
SECRECY Shrouds the rights of humanity as the
        torturers are set free to live while good men
        are jailed for speaking truth to power.

Generals cower thirsty for control. Standing and lying even
as the truth
    is unfold.
    Totalitarian plight against the light of freedom
    and the beacon of hope lost far in the fog out of
    lens and scope.

Ludicrous debt of the not so great generation, stratospheric
    escalation of the Ponzi scheme dissemination. The

future youth is facing extermination.

    These poor old fools allowed themselves to get mugged

    and now feed off of the credit of those who have barely

    begun.

WE THE YOUTH

        Stand strong in opposition. Freedom and prosperity

            our position.

MESSAGES OF REVOLUTION

Revolution sparked by all that is being kept in the dark.

Sanitized population cleansed by popular corporate indoctrination. They steal the nations wealth & health with no consequence or explanation.

Mutated organisms created for profit while gods creations are destroyed in the name of progress. Arrogance of man taken full flight, humanity and respect for life desecrated.

A system devoid of integrity.
Freedom
lost to fear and totalitarian aspirations. Tyrannical reverberations rule our sacred interpretations.

Judges of the regime strip the slaves of persecution
without just cause simply because it offers power
to the idle weak cowards with superficial titles.
Freedom withers in the presence of this malignant essence. Its very existence a defilement of all love and harmony. Universal rules violated natural law obliterated.

As we enter the abyss I wonder this while I walk with spirits and I talk to ghosts in a cloud of smoke trying to stoke fires of the host. Will we ever be free?

Weapons confiscated our only resort denied.
Convictions derived from pain and suffering. Despair
swells in the hearts of the betrayed. Dismayed hopes of the
sun to rise but only
darkness fills in our enemies eyes
                                              filled
                          with
                                    lies.

TYRANTS OF RANK

Leadership of corruption, rights and justice on the plate for
        their consumption. A panopticon prison
   these
traitors destroy all for their prism.
        Brave individuals sacrifice life, fortune and
   sacred
honor in order to secure freedom from those of fodder.
        Government insiders nothing more than
   traitors who
dishonor, wearing brass and title as if supreme rights from
        god have been bestowed. We the people
   should see
        them beaten and dethroned. For their
   treasonous
violation a revolution is brewing.
        Despite peaceful hesitation there seems to be
   no
        other solution only empty hands with no
restitution.

Throne of Creation

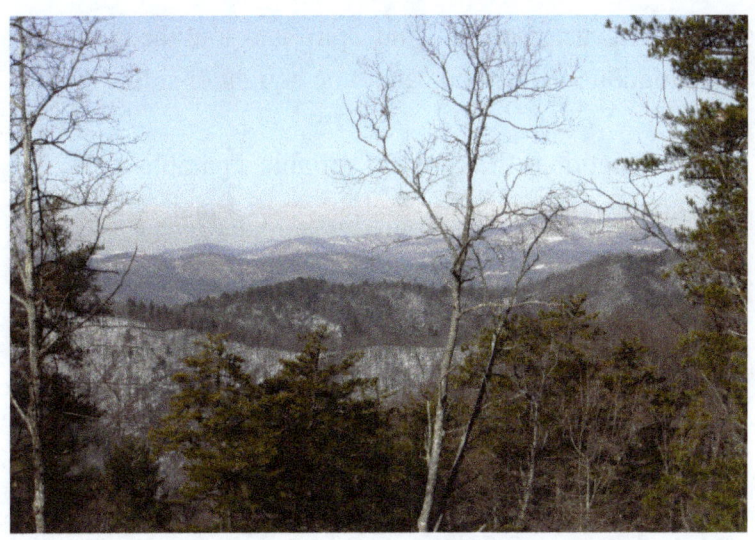

For all that sits at the throne of creation and all that we are as species among all of earths other populations.

Tolerance in the name of coexistence, divine liberty states there is no need for extinction.

Bountiful harvest of choice endless varieties of natural selection what seeds we plant are our own election.

Freedom is the child of choice and liberty a tribe of individuals with independent clarity.

All life within our sphere shares the sovereign right to be here. Integrity for all states of being no mutations or engineering.

Universal spirit transcendence of the message ancients have been trying to send us.

Ascension of the mind, spirit and soul the glory of this kingdom understood cannot be bought or sold.

Election is the constant variable a parable quite comparable to infinity. An endless parallel plain within all that cannot be explained.

A definition is not to be had. No limitations or confinements an expression best left incomplete, free from defilement.

At the throne of creation sits all that is free to choose from an infinite variety of outcomes.

Liberty is the divine dove sent to govern. Destiny, freedom, love are all choices given from the
throne
high above.

Prophets

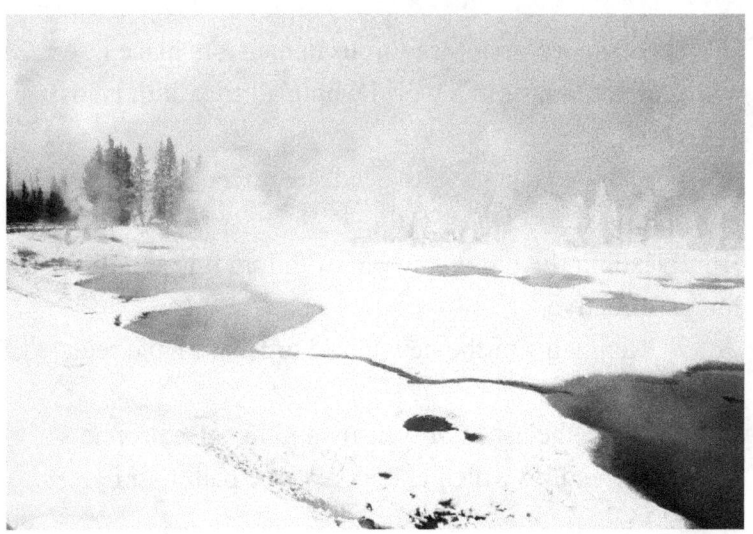

Prophets seeking, prophets speaking, prophets profiteering but not for those who are hearing.

Search carefully for all that you seek for it may find you. In the good rest blessed, in the wrong eternally distressed.

No respect without intellect. Homicidal ignorance in the name of god we must reject. With these words I take a stand and defect against those who violence project.

Hollow, empty thrones of prophets with no faith speaking to the poor, false promises nothing more.

Words for the world of the meek if the world they are to inherent than it must be made   apparent that there is

no *declarant* above them other than the lords blessing.
It is the very thing the oppressors are cursing.

Blasphemers of traitorous demeanors place interest
above all at all cost in a world where all true faith is lost.

Value perspective twisted superficial material
objective.
Blind leading the blind, a world of failure this paradigm no
longer effective.
Remnants of the new world order we have rejected.

From the ashes of tyranny and its false prophets
shall rise freedom which is the only true path to progress.

Superficial plains of existence not nearly enough to
express the distance.

The light of liberty will not be extinguished. It remains
bright in a sea of darkness, quite distinguished.

SOLUTIONS

Blood and violence are better solutions than a world of
silence.

A world unraveled where is the gavel? There is no
justice let us adjust this!

Step into my mind. I will show you all that lies
behind the curtain of these things I am certain.

Cosmically searching for universal truth. Our place
is small but destiny is true.

Questions may be asked albeit the answers do not
last. We must appreciate the obvious if we are to truly
understand all that is above us.

Freedoms love and consequence were given to all
of Eden's innocence. Mans toil and struggle self-induced
formerly perfect now reduced. Fallen from grace forced to
find their own place.

Those who follow the path lit by the anointment of
his holy appointment will walk in peace and in his spirit
never cease.

A world of questions with so few answers. So many
diseases and disaster. So much pain and so little shame,
bitterly cold our sin never gets old.

Searching for answers in a world which is encroaching the wings of freedom are being clipped by men of sin, darkness is approaching.

Serpents of oppression wishing to erase god and his impressions.

There are no solutions to the polluted spirit of man only regressions of his arrogant plans which illuminate the humility of his genius and capable hands.

Iron Fist

Iron fist crushing all that it grips, all power from men does it strip.

Refusing to open never lending a hand it cares not for man only control of the land.

Absolute power the fist rules over every hour. No escape from its clutches it breaks independence and leaves it in crutches.

A society handicapped and crippled of liberty not a tiny wave or ripple.

What justice could not heal god and war will repeal.

From the iron fist arose a single son, standing in defiance now the war has begun. Before you pull the trigger at my brain, my words will remain the same; Death before dishonor!

For each free soul who knows their place is small yet their destiny true an iron fist is incapable of containing you.

Breaking free from social oppression your choices infinite never at their discretion.

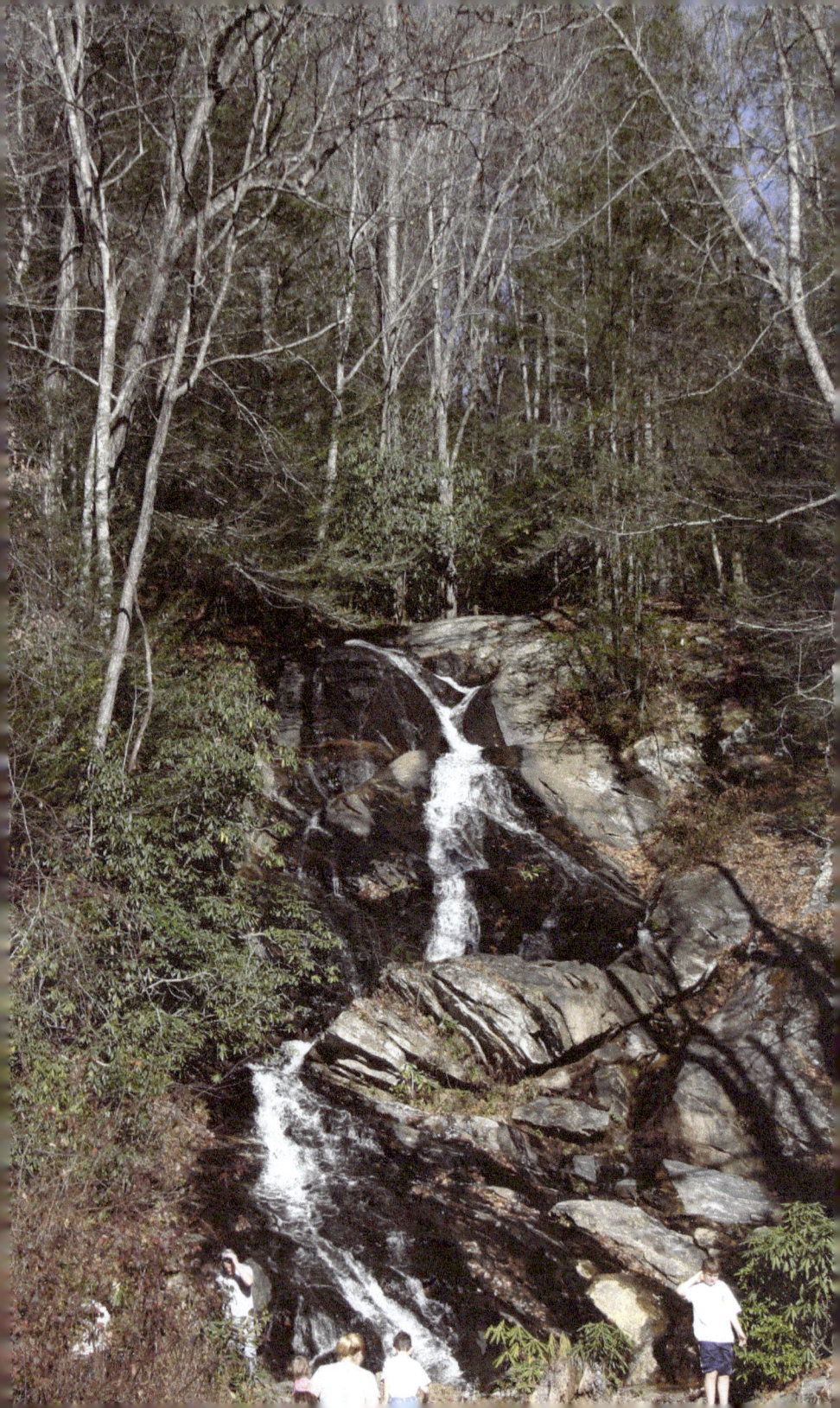

Not Alone

Spirit of man and his flesh incarnate the divine spirits of this place never discarded.

Not alone in this world filled with magic and mystery divine contact alone etched in stone our ancient history.

The repository of mans spirit runs deeper in time than most would like to acknowledge. The heart of creation itself is in us out of the depths of our souls we must dredge it.

None of liberties sons are alone. Split a piece of wood, think of love and return to your essence so that you may see yourself as a rich man in anyone's presence.

You cannot define but you can try to find what lies behind. You may not leave empty handed in some ways you may understand it.

Release inhibitions there are no prohibitions on the sacrament, every once in a while drink much more than this.

If for nothing else always celebrate you are not alone; you are one of the flock, one of our own.

Sedated Nation

A nation of sedated minds sold encapsulated poison in order to put it behind.

Reality subdued, substance abused a sedated nation so sad and confused.

Existence so entrapped and unamused a system that requires you to be subdued.

Normalcy biased perspective, everything new unique or different is rejected.

Conformity an obligation we are the sedated nation.

Minds numbed out to quell the discontent which leads to doubt. Our spring of fulfillment run dry always living in drought.

Villainous Invasion, theses drugs incite a murderous citation. Young minds seeking relief from the growing pains of their disbelief refusing to accept the world for its joy and grief.

Pharmaceutical empires lobbying associations to further expand disassociations within the definitions of the human minds conditions all in the name of monetary ambitions.

A nation empty and hollow all are given a pill to

swallow. In an unnatural state of being we are forced to alter feelings about the world we are seeing.

A sedated nation eternally prescribed drugs far worse than any symptoms described.

Police State

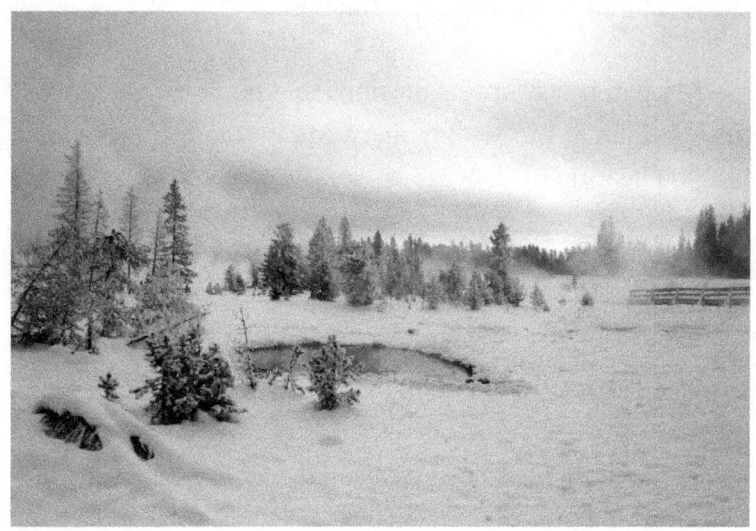

A police state of intimidation this is about much more than racial oppression. Freedom is the goal and obsession.

Submit to arrest or be put to the test. Ultimate authority to make you bleed if their commands you fail to heed.

Black, whites and brown! PENEMUE is telling you how it goes down!
Respect to the citizenry will be paid or every unjust authority will be slain.

A pen is mightier than a sword. May my words cut through an incision of exact precision, "non-violent! non-violent!", never in prison.

I ask citizens at large to take charge.
Demand action and in liberty create a grand faction we are
the greater number they are a fraction.

My pen is a sword its meaning and purpose you will
absorb. I am at war with tyranny. Many statements made,
are you hearing me?

Individuals keep the faith! Institutions always mistake
their place.

The pen is mightier than the sword a sacred oath I have
sworn.
Freedom has been weakened and diluted our society
sickened and polluted.

A house of pain under duress and strain when will
we live in peace and refrain from the violence of these
chains.

Issues

I speak about issues when I show up they need tissues.
Subjects that rip to the soul of it. Life demands a
great toll wit.

Same old world everyday getting worse, struggling
and striving to show the world your worth.

Opportunities given! World is your oyster. Everyday
is thanksgiving trying to give back to those who are hunger
driven.

Issues pounding at my door my brothers being taken
and killed I can't take this shit anymore.

PENEMUE speaking up about the human condition.
This is my poetic rendition.

Issues rule the day how long does it stay?
So many books I've read dictating how my pen has bled.
From the truth of knowledge tyranny has always fled.

Issues flowing through my veins, my eyes befall the
world so tarnished and stained. Its grace must be fought for
and maintained if the future is to be free of this pressure
and pain.

Refuse your social inoculation pure blooded human
beings the world is flooded with so many disturbing things.

Accept good and evil for what they are in your heart and you will never be set apart.

Fear the ultimate tool for compliance, respect no longer a part of the equation, absolute power rules every occasion.

Suffocating us with their collective weakness, in the name of independence we the people   must speak on this.

Issues, injustice issuing, these events will not keep continuing.

Peel back the wool from your eyes. Reveal your teeth and be wise.

We the people will rule and survive.